Secrets of the Stars

15 BEDTIME STORIES INSPIRED BY NATURE

Contents

4 When the Sun Goes Down...

6 The Adventure Begins

14 Night Flyers

16 The Glowing Eyes

24 Night Swimmers

26 Keep on Rolling

34 Small but Mighty

36 Adventures by Starlight

44 A Blue Spectacle

46 Sounds of the Sahara

54 Desert Dwellers

56 Training in the Tundra

64 Meet the Pack

66 Home, Sweet Home

74 A Friendly Burrower

76 A Wild Winter Chase

84 What a Hoot!

86 Learning from the Expert
   94 Smelly, Strong, and Savage

96 Who Glows There?
   104 Life on the Reef

106 Blooms at Bedtime
   114 Desert Giants

116 The Pizza Heist
   124 A Creature of Many Talents

126 The Night Flight
   134 The Circle of Life

136 Hide-and-Seek
   144 Beware: Flying Frogs

146 The Bushbaby Babies
   154 Petite Primates

   156 Glossary
   158 Index
   160 Acknowledgements

When the Sun Goes Down...

While you are sleeping, many animals are awake. From the Arctic to Australia, nocturnal creatures live their lives under the cover of darkness. They find food, raise families, and even have adventures! You'll discover some of these amazing animals in the tales in this book. This map shows where each story is set.

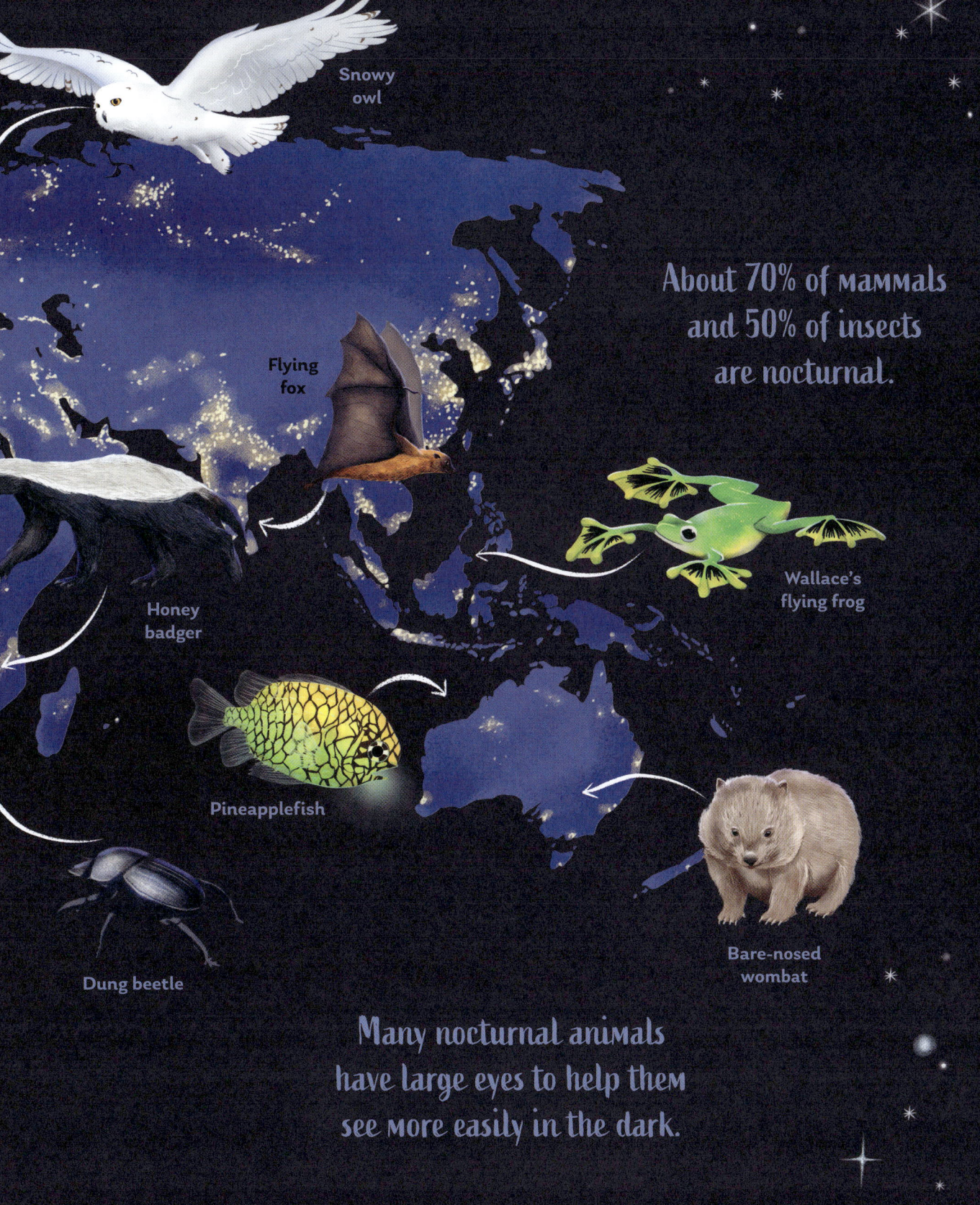

About 70% of mammals and 50% of insects are nocturnal.

Snowy owl
Flying fox
Honey badger
Wallace's flying frog
Pineapplefish
Dung beetle
Bare-nosed wombat

Many nocturnal animals have large eyes to help them see more easily in the dark.

The Adventure Begins

The sun is setting over a lake in southern India. Its orange streaks stretch through the branches of a banyan tree. This change in light seems to bring the tree to life like a natural alarm clock. **SQUEALS** and **SQUAWKS** fill the air. The sounds are coming from large brown lumps hanging from the branches. What are these noisy lumps? They're thousands of Indian flying foxes that call the banyan tree their home!

The flying foxes start to rise and shine. Each releases its grip on a branch and takes to the sky. But one flying fox is a little slower to get started. Her chocolate brown eyes scope out the scene. She unwraps her leathery wings from around her body. As she does, a surprise reveals itself – she's got a big belly. She is going to have a baby soon! She is also *very* hungry.

She removes her sharp claws from the smooth bark before taking off. Her wide wings sound heavy as she flies. **FLAP! FLAP! FLAP!** Soon she's halfway across the glass-like surface of the lake. The water looks inviting. Time for a quick belly dip! She dives down with a little splash. The cool water feels refreshing after snoozing in the sun all day.

By the time the sun has set, the sky is like a painter's canvas. But instead of drops of paint, thousands of stars glitter like diamonds. They twinkle and shine. There's no sign of the moon on this early April night. Over the next few hours, the flying fox uses her eyes and nose to find food. She feasts on fruit and flowers. By the time she returns to her roosting tree, she has flown several miles. Even though she is weary, she doesn't dare land on one of the upper branches of the banyan. Those belong to the most powerful males. Instead, she finds a mid-level branch where she can relax in peace.

After waiting several months for her baby to arrive, it is finally time for the flying fox to give birth. Having a baby in a treetop is no small feat!

The pup arrives feet first and grabs on to its mum straightaway. It has a furry coat and wide-open eyes. The new mum is very careful to make sure her pup doesn't fall. She cradles and nurses her baby.

The tiny flying fox grows quickly. In its first weeks, it grabs on to a branch with its feet and flaps wildly without going anywhere. Sometimes its mum carries it on foraging trips at night. Tonight is one of those times! With her pup, the flying fox mum soars across the starry night sky. They feed on flowers. Occasionally, they eat an insect or two. But fruit is their favourite food. After eating the fruit they spit out the seeds and dry pulp. **PTOO! PTOO!**

The days grow blisteringly hot as monsoon season arrives. The mum and her baby often fan their wings, then lick their wrists to cool down. Sometimes the night sky lights up with flashes of lightning. The rain pelts down on the banyan tree and all of its residents. It feels heavenly!

For a couple of months, the flying fox mum continues to bring her pup to foraging sites. But once there, the pup flies on its own. It covers the short distance between branches in search of a banana or juicy mango. The next month, something big happens. Instead of waiting for the pup to climb on to her, the mum flies off from the banyan tree by herself. **SWOOSH!** She watches, waiting to see what will happen next...

Beneath a cloudy sky, the flying fox pup lets go of the bark, and soars into the sky! It catches up to its mum and flies close to her, ready for the new adventures the night will bring.

What's on the menu?

Indian flying foxes belong to a group of big bats called megabats. Their diet is mainly fruit, though they also eat flowers and nectar. They only occasionally eat insects. Most of the world's bats are microbats, which are smaller.

Night Flyers

Indian flying foxes are native to southern Asia. They often live in tropical forests and swamps. These furry-faced mammals can have a wingspan of 1.2–1.5 m (4–5 ft) long. The ones in this story live in the state of Tamil Nadu in southern India.

Seed spreaders

When Indian flying foxes feed and fly around, they pollinate plants and spread seeds in their poo. This helps new flowers, fruits, and trees grow in the habitats where the flying foxes live. It's a win for the bats and the environment!

Bats are the only mammals in the world that fly.

THE SCIENCE BEHIND THE STORY

Vampire bat

Bloodsucking vampires

Vampire bats are famous for drinking the blood of animals to survive. It sounds scary, but this often doesn't even harm their prey. In fact, sometimes the animal that the bat is feeding from doesn't even wake up!

Bats or foxes?

Indian flying foxes are one of the world's largest bats. They were given their name because their fuzzy heads look a bit like foxes.

Wonderful wings

The bone structure of a flying fox's wing is similar to a person's hand. Long, delicate finger bones stretch outwards from its wrist. These bones create the frame, which gives support to the membrane that allows this furry creature to fly.

The Glowing Eyes

You arrive at Everglades National Park after dark.
You turn on your torch and follow your guide to the entrance of the Anhinga Trail. Once there, you turn off the light. It takes a minute or two for your eyes to adjust to the darkness. The sky is a velvety shade between deep purple and black. Despite the late hour, a warm, gentle breeze grazes your cheek.

Before you get very far, a low, grunting sound repeats over and over again. **OINK! OINK! OINK!** Could there be a pig on the trail? As you creep along you discover the real culprits – pig frogs! These amphibians are hunting for tasty beetles. Feeding at night is safer, since the wading birds that hunt them are much less active then.

You borrow some night vision binoculars from your dad and look at the branches of a pond apple tree in the distance. As you focus the binoculars, a great egret comes into view. Its bright white feathers stand out against the night sky. The egret is sleeping peacefully.

You continue down the trail. The air smells moist, as if you're in a greenhouse. Something on the ground is glowing. It looks like two green eyes are on the path just ahead of you. You speed-walk to see if you can catch up with the phantom eyes. But right as you are about to get within striking distance, something goes **CLICK!** And just like that, the eyes vanish – as suddenly as they appeared. Spooky!

Other creatures soon appear on the boardwalk. A southern leopard frog hops by. It hurries past in the direction of chuckling sounds. Perhaps the frog is on its way to find a mate in the wetland next to the path.

Barely a moment later, you almost trip over two bright green streaks racing across the path. What are these whizzing wonders? They're lizards called green anoles, one of which is being chased! He soon grabs on to a palm tree not far off the trail. Once there, he shows off his red throat pouch. He's sending a message to any other males: *Want to fight? I'm game!*

Not all the nighttime activity is happening on the ground. When you look up at the starry sky, something is darting above the walkway. Its silhouette is faint. The mysterious tiny creature is a Florida bonneted bat. It dips and dances on its hunt for mosquitoes.

What other mysteries does this night have in store? Curious, you stand perfectly still in the middle of the walkway. A watery wonderland lies all around you. The wind rustles faraway reeds. Large logs float on the water's surface.

Deep bellows come from the water. **CROAK! CROAK!** Despite the dim light, you search for the source of the throaty tones. That's when you notice something strange. Bright red stars seem to shine on the distant water. Are you the only one noticing these red stars?

You're about to ask your family when the craziest series of events begins…

A great blue heron swoops down. It tries to grab one of the southern chorus frogs whose rasping trills have been filling the air. But then, one of the floating logs lurches forwards. **SPLASH!!!** That is no log! It has a mouth full of super-sharp teeth. And those red stars aren't stars either. They are the shining eyes of… an American alligator!

The alligator tries to grab the heron, thinking it would make a good midnight feast. Unfortunately for the reptile, its lurch is a second too late. The heron makes a speedy exit. Your heart races at all the excitement happening only metres in front of you. You turn to your mum. "Can we come back again tomorrow?" you plead. She smiles at you and nods. "Absolutely – I want to see what creatures are around during the day too!"

THE SCIENCE BEHIND THE STORY

Night Swimmers

American alligators are native to the southeast USA. They are commonly found in some freshwater rivers, but also live in marshes, swamps, and lakes. These giant reptiles can occasionally reach 4.5 m (15 ft) long. The ones in this story live in Everglades National Park in Florida.

Extraordinary eyes

At the back of an alligator's eye is a special structure. This structure gives them better night vision and makes their eyes glow red when reflecting the limited light at night. Cats have the same structure, which is why their eyes also shine at night!

Refill, please!

Sometimes an American alligator's teeth fall out. Other times they get worn down. When this happens, they are swiftly replaced with new teeth.

Home sweet home

The habitat where American alligators live can affect their colouring. For example, adults living in waters with a lot of algae have greener skin than those living in areas with overhanging trees.

Over the course of an American alligator's life, it can go through as many as 3,000 teeth!

Mystery solved

The mysterious "eyes" that appear on the path in this story belong to a click beetle. But they aren't really eyes. Instead, they are two glowing nodes on the beetle's thorax – the middle section of their body. They don't flash like a firefly, but brighten and dim instead.

Keep on Rolling

It's a moonless night in South Africa. The air is still, the temperature mild. A dazzle of zebras **SNORT** and **WHUFF** at each other. They're using their teeth to pull out some loose hairs and give each other a nice scratch. Ahhh...

A long, narrow purple and mauve cloud stretches as far as the eye can see. Beneath this magical-looking cloud is a bright band of light. Zillions of stars fleck the heavens.

Far below, a zebra poos. **PLOP! PLOP! PLOP!** Its dung is dry and has a grassy scent. This is thrilling to a nearby African dung beetle. It waggles its antennae, trying to pinpoint the location of the smell. Soon, loads of these beetles race to the scene. And they are excited. Why? Piles of poo mean it's time to eat!

Our dung beetle quickly begins to tear off pieces of poo. His front legs push one chunk at a time into a blob. Then, like a sculptor, he shapes the pieces into a perfect ball. *Voilà* – his masterpiece is complete! Satisfied with his edible sculpture, our dung beetle starts to climb his creation. When he reaches the top he looks up at the glorious night sky, before rotating his body around. He is dancing! He spins around, making one more complete circle, before returning to the ground.

The African dung beetle heads away from the chaotic scene at the poo pile. He moves backwards in a straight line, rolling his food ball along with his back feet. The whole time he's moving he can't see where he's going! Not far into the journey, another male approaches. What does he want? The poo ball, of course! This rival tries to dislodge our hard-working beetle from his ball. It's a beetle battle!

Both males rise up on their hind legs. Each uses its forelegs to try to hammer the other around the head. **SMASH! BANG! OOMPH!** The dung beetles barely notice when a couple of brown hyenas run by. The hyenas are not interested in the beetles. They're chasing some rodents for a nighttime snack.

Our beetle knocks his opponent off balance. He sprints back to his ball to keep rolling. The hopeful thief pursues him for a while, running as fast as his legs can go. Eventually the rival decides he is not going to win the battle. He slinks off, hoping he'll be able to steal another male's loot.

It's a tough slog rolling such a heavy ball across uneven ground. The poo ball weighs far more than the beetle himself. He passes over pebbles. Over fallen sticks. He skirts a watering hole, nearly falling in. **WHEW!** That was a close call!

By this point the tiny beetle has been on the move for a while and is getting weary. He has moved his precious cargo about two hundred metres from where the zebra left its poo pile. Rather than keep rolling, he decides he's far enough away from his competitors now. Despite all his hard work, there's still one more job to do. It's time to dig!

Our African dung beetle digs a tunnel in the dirt beneath him. Soil flies all around. He wants to hide his dung ball as quickly as possible.

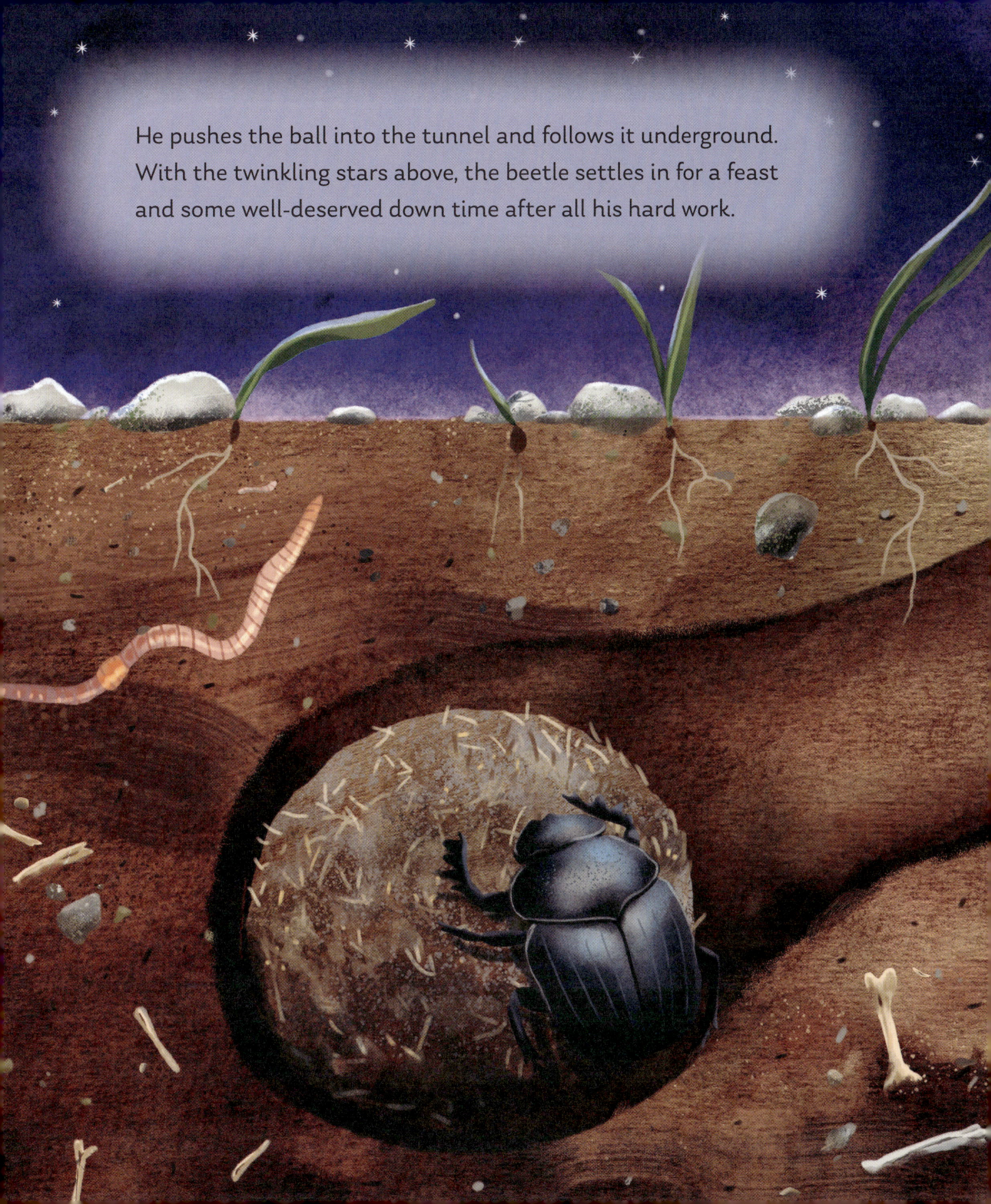
He pushes the ball into the tunnel and follows it underground. With the twinkling stars above, the beetle settles in for a feast and some well-deserved down time after all his hard work.

An African dung beetle's brain is the size of a poppy seed.

Beetle astronomer

The bright stripe of light in the night sky in this story is part of the Milky Way – the galaxy that we live in! When the dung beetle looks up at the stripe (from the top of its poo ball), it turns itself at an angle to that stripe. Then the beetle holds that angle as it rolls away, allowing it to move in a straight line. The beetle is acting as an astronomer to help guide its way!

Singular stripes

Every zebra has its own unique pattern of stripes, just like a person's fingerprint. Some scientists have suggested that zebras may be able to identify one another by their stripes.

Recycling champions

Although small, dung beetles have a huge impact on the environments where they live. They efficiently recycle poo by both burying and eating it. This process helps to keep the soil healthy.

THE SCIENCE BEHIND THE STORY

Small but Mighty

There are about 9,500 species of dung beetles in the world. They live on all continents except Antarctica. The ones in this story are African dung beetles. They live near the town of Vryburg, about 250 miles (400 km) from Johannesburg, South Africa.

Power pushers

Dung beetles are known for being incredibly strong. The ones that roll their poo balls often move balls that are 10 to 20 times bigger than themselves! The strongest of them all are the male taurus scarab beetles (another kind of dung beetle) that can pull more than 1,100 times their body weight. That's like a person being able to pull the weight of six double-decker buses!

Dancing in the dark

African dung beetles dance for a reason. By rotating their bodies around once or twice on top of their poo balls, they can determine the direction they want to travel in before they carry on rolling.

Adventures by Starlight

On a clear summer evening, a young male indigo bunting looks up at the sky. He is perched on a tree branch at the edge of a field. Far below, cicadas **BUZZ** and crickets **CHIRP**. Their songs fill the air.

Night after night, the bunting studies the patterns of the stars above. Some twinkle. Others are faint. One part of the night sky is especially interesting to the little bird. The bunting is captivated by the very bright North Star. It is located right at the end of the tail of the bear in the constellation Ursa Minor.

Throughout the summer, the bunting feasts on bugs and berries. The overgrown field nearby is rich in tasty treats! But soon the days grow shorter. He moults and so do all the birds around him. The adult males shed their brilliant blue feathers. Their new ones are tawny like his own. Some birds around him change colour more quickly than others. Finally, on a clear night in early October, our little bunting decides the time is right. He's ready to start a huge journey southwards. Once again, he studies the stars.

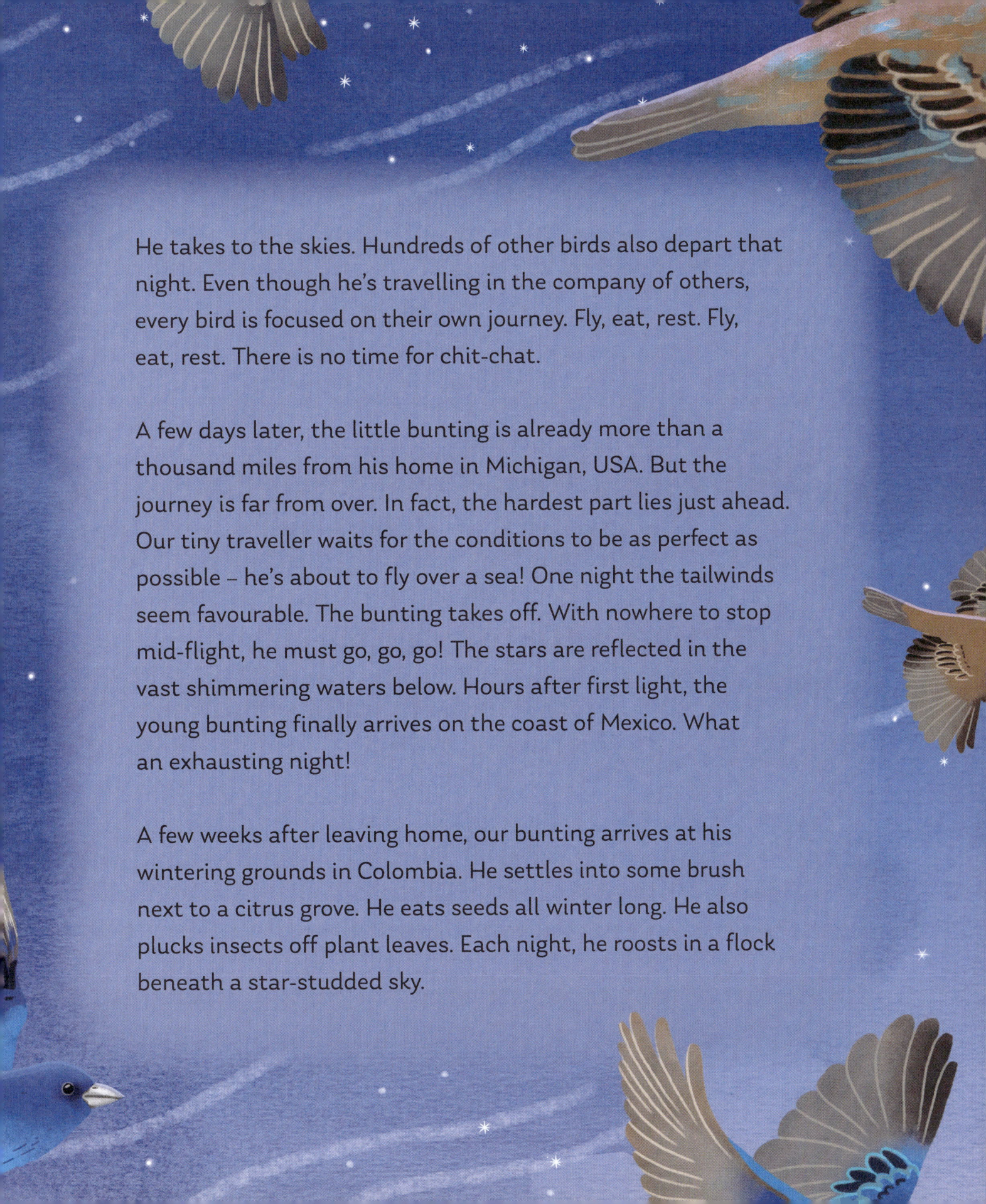

He takes to the skies. Hundreds of other birds also depart that night. Even though he's travelling in the company of others, every bird is focused on their own journey. Fly, eat, rest. Fly, eat, rest. There is no time for chit-chat.

A few days later, the little bunting is already more than a thousand miles from his home in Michigan, USA. But the journey is far from over. In fact, the hardest part lies just ahead. Our tiny traveller waits for the conditions to be as perfect as possible – he's about to fly over a sea! One night the tailwinds seem favourable. The bunting takes off. With nowhere to stop mid-flight, he must go, go, go! The stars are reflected in the vast shimmering waters below. Hours after first light, the young bunting finally arrives on the coast of Mexico. What an exhausting night!

A few weeks after leaving home, our bunting arrives at his wintering grounds in Colombia. He settles into some brush next to a citrus grove. He eats seeds all winter long. He also plucks insects off plant leaves. Each night, he roosts in a flock beneath a star-studded sky.

Gradually, winter turns to spring. The days get longer. In March, our bunting starts to moult again. This year, most of the feathers that come in are blue. He leaves his wintering grounds in April. The arduous journey back to Michigan involves another flight over the choppy waters between Mexico and the USA.

The rhythms of our indigo bunting's year are like clockwork. Summers in Michigan and winters in Colombia. Two years after his birth, the now sapphire-coloured bird returns for what will be an eventful summer. He arrives in a forest clearing. He's looking for a place to call his own before the females arrive.

He spends much of his summer days singing, hoping to attract a mate. CHIRP! CHIRP! Our beautiful bunting's sweet melodies eventually catch the attention of a female. He really wants to impress her so he uses more than just music. He puts on quite a show! First, he struts in circles in front of the female. Then he spreads his wings and ducks his head down.

The female likes his moves. Hurray! She decides she will be his partner. During their courtship period, he follows his mate around. He watches as she crafts a beautiful cup-shaped nest from grass, weeds, and strips of bark. It takes her eight days to construct this nest.

After the nest is built, the female is ready to lay eggs. The male stays with her. Not long after sunrise, she lays one white egg in the nest. She repeats this for three days in a row. Once the eggs are in the nest, the male returns to his solitary ways. The female keeps the eggs warm for almost two weeks. Then – **CRACK! PEEP!** The chicks emerge! The female feeds the hatchlings until they are old enough to leave the nest. Soon these young fledglings will study the night sky too, preparing for the time when they will have nighttime adventures of their own.

THE SCIENCE BEHIND THE STORY

A Blue Spectacle

During spring migration and breeding season, indigo buntings are often found in the eastern half of the USA. They migrate to winter in southern Florida, and from central Mexico down to northern South America. The ones in this story migrate between Michigan, USA, and Colombia.

Colour changers

Male indigo buntings do not start life with vibrant blue feathers. In their first year, they can range from having mostly brown and white feathers with just a little blue to being much more blue. It typically takes two years for males to reach their most brilliant shade of blue.

Sometimes indigo buntings use spider webs to bind their nests together.

No turning back

An especially hard part of an indigo bunting's migration is crossing the gulf between the USA and Mexico. There aren't any landing spots so the birds have to rely on tailwinds (strong winds blowing in the same direction they're flying in) to get across in just one night. Luckily, these tiny migrants are terrific weather forecasters.

Guided by the stars

Before their first migration, young indigo buntings study the night sky. They focus their attention on the area near the North Star. By learning the patterns of stars in the northern sky, indigo buntings are able to navigate accurately. Not bad for little birds!

Ursa Minor

North Star

What a tune!

Young indigo buntings learn the songs they sing from males that live nearby. Male buntings in what's called a "song neighbourhood" sing almost identical songs. They might sing the same song for as long as 20 years, and the song will change gradually as new singers put their own twists on it over time.

Sounds of the Sahara

Dusk is falling over the Sahara Desert. Wind rushes through the tall dunes. Grains of sand whizz in all directions. The sounds attract the attention of an animal whose den lies at the foot of the dunes. It's time to rise and shine!

Our mystery creature wonders what's happening above its sandy home. It chatters to its den mates. Its huge ears turn to and fro. Before it ventures out for the night, it licks some dew that has formed inside its den. *Yum* – that always hits the spot!

Who is this curious creature? It's a fennec fox!

SNAP! CRACKLE! These sounds tell the fox that breakfast might be close by. The fox wriggles her way up and out of her den. Her ears rotate again as she works to get a lay of the land. It doesn't take long to pinpoint where the snaps and crackles are coming from.

The fox darts across the desert, nearly invisible thanks to her reddish cream-coloured fur that camouflages perfectly with the sand. The fox soon reaches a patch of spiny zilla. Her ears tell her something is hiding amid the pinkish-violet flowers. The fennec fox circles the plant, listening all the while. Who is making the noise? It's a desert locust. The fox quickly roots out the insect. Then, **CRUNCH!** What a tasty start to the evening.

POP! POP! POP! What's this sound coming from the sand? The fox immediately starts digging with all four paws. Tufts of grass and sand fly into the air. The fox exposes a scorpion! She seems unafraid of the fierce-looking arachnid. The scorpion comes at the fox, with tail raised and pincers spread wide. *Yikes!*

For several minutes, the fox moves like a boxer. She lunges at the scorpion, then darts back when the scorpion gets too close to her face. Advance. Retreat. Advance. Retreat.

With her enormous ears flattened behind her head, the fox grips the scorpion by the tail. She throws the scorpion up and down against the sand. **SPLAT! SPOOF!**

The fox wins the battle and starts munching. She's careful to bite off the scorpion's tail first so that she doesn't get stung.

A little later, the fennec fox senses danger. A Pharaoh eagle-owl silently swoops down. Could it be the fox's turn to be on the menu? The fox shrieks. She zigs, zags, and jumps in an attempt to lose the owl. Luckily, her furry paws give her great grip on the sand. With the owl's talons almost reaching her black-tipped tail, the fox just barely manages to dive into her den. That was close!

The fox rests a bit after her frightening encounter. Then she scampers back into the Sahara to try her luck again. In no time, the fox hears **PITTER-PATTER, PITTER-PATTER**. The sound is coming from underground. Time to dig again.

The source of the sound is a jerboa! The tiny rodent squeals. It kicks up sand as it tries to hide. Some ends up in the fox's face. The jerboa has another trick up its sleeve: powerful, kangaroo-like legs. The jerboa hops off in a flash! The fox gives chase, her lean body streaming over the dunes. Even though the fox is a faster sprinter, the jerboa manages to slip away. Not every hunt can be a success.

What other sounds does the fox detect during her evening foraging? The slithering of a Sahara sand viper. The hopping of a gerbil. And as the sun starts to rise above the dunes, the fox hears and smells other animals who are just beginning their day. **DEE DJRRUU** calls a desert wheatear mid-flight. Its morning whistles remind the fox that it's time to head home. Back in her den, she settles and drifts off to sleep.

Desert Dwellers

Fennec foxes live throughout North Africa and eastward into the Sinai and Arabian Peninsulas. The fennec fox in this story lives in the Sahara Desert of Libya.

Furry and fast

The bottoms of a fennec fox's feet are covered in dense hair. This protects their soles from the scorching desert sands. These fuzzy feet can really zip along. Fennec foxes can run at speeds of up to 20 mph (32 kph)!

Fennec foxes are the smallest members of the dog family.

THE SCIENCE BEHIND THE STORY

Nature's architects

Fennec foxes commonly build their dens at the base of sand dunes because the firmer sand makes it easier for the foxes to construct a safe burrow. They often dig a series of tunnels. A den may have several exits and entrances to give the foxes more escape routes.

No drinks on the menu

Fennec foxes can go for a long time without drinking water. They get the hydration they need from the food that they eat. Their diet includes insects, rodents, birds (and their eggs), and lizards. Roots, leaves, and fruits are also good sources of water.

Locust

Lizard

A fennec fox's ears are nearly one half the length of its body, not counting its tail!

Enormous ears

Fennec foxes are famous for their huge ears, which can reach 15 cm (6 in). These giant ears allow them to hear prey underground. They also work as built-in air conditioners. A network of veins runs through their ears, which cools their blood and helps to lower their body temperature. Nifty, huh?

Training in the Tundra

AHH-WOOOOO! As a pack of grey wolves howls, the sound carries across the vast tundra. It's nearly midnight, yet the sun is just setting here in the Yukon, northwest Canada. Four young wolf cubs emerge from their den. They are curious about the sounds around them. Although these bundles of fluff were born nearly two months ago, they are only starting to explore their surroundings.

The pups chase each other, enjoying the wolf version of tag. They are easily distracted by almost anything that appears on their path. A patch of cottongrass swaying gently. A willow ptarmigan roosting under a bush. Some dwarf birch leaves fluttering just above the ground. There's so much to see and smell!

One pup finds a pile of bones from a recent hunt. He picks one up in his teeth and carries it around. One of his siblings growls and tries to steal it, starting a game of tug-of-war! The other pups practise their best hunting moves. They're too busy to notice their mum taking off!

While the wolf mum is gone, the pups are in safe hands. Another member of the pack has arrived to babysit. She keeps a close eye on them. The pups yap as they roam. One starts to stray a little too far from the den. The babysitter grabs him by his neck. She is trying to flip him over onto his back, but the sassy cub barks at her and refuses to cooperate. **OWW! WHIM! YAP!** Eventually she pins the pup down. He doesn't bark this time so the babysitter lets him back up. The pup has learned his lesson.

Several hours later, the mother wolf returns from her outing. As she approaches, the pups smell something delicious. It's beaver meat. The pups wrestle one another, each hoping to get its fair share. They feast beneath the starry sky. With full bellies, they head into their den to flop for a rest.

The pups grow bigger and stronger during the summer. Pouncing on a sibling's tail or chasing a red-backed vole is part fun and part skill development. Some nights the pups add something sweet to their diet – fresh blueberries. **CHOMP!** Their muzzles, stained purple, give away their secret snack. What a treat!

Autumn turns to winter. The wolf pups travel further afield with their mum and the pack. High above, the sky is awash with the electric green swirls of the northern lights. The wolves howl loudly when another pack enters their territory. They're saying: *back off!*

One night, an ermine zooms past. As it zigs and zags among the low shrubs, one wolf pup follows. In her haste to catch the ermine, the pup runs away from the pack.

AHH-WOOOOO! The lost pup howls and howls. She hopes the pack will hear her cries for help. But the pack is many miles away now. Unfortunately, the pup's cries for help attract the attention of some other wolves in the vicinity. The lost pup catches a whiff of these other wolves. Their smell tells her that these are not her pack members. She quickly scampers away from the scent!

Days pass. The lost pup looks for safe places to snooze. A mat of soft moss makes a cosy bed. Without her mum and the pack around, the pup is forced to test out her hunting skills. One night she manages to catch some lemmings. But on another food-finding mission, she comes up short. Her belly rumbles. Will she ever find her pack?

A crescent moon dimly lights the tundra. Light snow begins to fall, frosting the lichens and shrubs with shimmering white crystals. Suddenly, the pup's ears perk up. She hears a familiar sound. **AHH-WOOOOO! AHH-WOOOOO!** Is it her mum? Could it be her pack? The lonesome pup howls back excitedly. Both pup and pack howl and sniff deeply to locate each other. The pup soon catches sight of her family. She sprints over rocks and plants. When she reaches her mum, she licks her muzzle. They rub their cheeks together. After their happy reunion, the pack takes off into the wilderness. Their next meal may be just around the corner…

What's in a howl?

Although wolves yelp, growl, bark, whimper, and yip, howls are the sound they are best known for. Howling serves many purposes. It can help a lost wolf find its pack. A pack can howl to let another pack know it is getting too close for comfort. Wolves also howl to strengthen the bond between pack members. Some howls can be heard from up to 10 miles (16 km) away!

A wolf can eat as much as 10 kg (22 lb) of meat in a single sitting. That's about the weight of a car tyre!

Meet the Pack

Grey wolves can be found in North America, Europe, and Asia. They are the biggest members of the dog family. They can thrive in a wide variety of habitats including mountains, forests, grasslands, and deserts. Grey wolves range in size from 1–2 m (4–7 ft) long. The ones in this story live in the tundra of Canada's Yukon province.

Strength in numbers

Wolf packs can range in size from as few as 2 to as many as 36 wolves. However, packs of 4 to 10 members are common. In the Yukon, the average pack size is between 7 and 9 wolves. A wolf pack is typically made up of a mated pair and their offspring. Some packs also include siblings of the breeding pair – the aunts and uncles of the pups.

THE SCIENCE BEHIND THE STORY

Pecking order

In order to survive, young wolf cubs have to learn their pack's rules. They must submit to the older wolves in the pack. Young wolves should never talk back to their elders! That's why the babysitter wolf in this story pins down the cub until he is quiet and obedient.

Not fussy eaters

The diet of grey wolves varies with the seasons. In the summer, they eat lots of beavers and berries (when available). In winter, they often eat moose.

Home, Sweet Home

Late at night, a bare-nosed wombat climbs out of her warren. Her seven-month-old joey is along for the ride, cosy in his pouch. The mother shuffles around, nibbling on on grass. But she doesn't forage for long. She's got a job to do! This busy wombat is building a new entrance to her burrow.

Her sharp claws get to work. First, she digs with her right paw. Then she switches sides. She uses her back legs to push the soil away, and it goes flying behind her. **SPLAT! SPLAT!** The joey watches the dirt whizz by from the comfort of his mum's pouch.

The pile of dirt grows and grows. When she decides it's big enough, the mother wombat backs up. As she pushes the soil behind her, it creates a ramp. At the same time, her joey drinks some of her milk in his pouch. The mum is doing two jobs at once!

After making good progress, the mum enjoys a well-deserved snack. The joey comes out to join her. They feed on tussock grass. Growling grass frogs call from a pond not far away. Right above mother and joey, a koala munches on eucalyptus leaves.

The wombat and joey decide to explore the forest. The mum eats a lot, and stops regularly to poo. But wait... her poo looks like cubes! She leaves nearly a hundred of them throughout her feeding territory during the night. On top of a newly fallen log, near the entrance to an echidna's burrow, on top of a pile of mushrooms... After walking for about a mile, the joey is weary. He climbs back into the pouch, ready for another rest. *ZZZZ*...

That night, an unexpected visitor arrives at the warren. It's a red fox! The mother wombat is not pleased. As the fox pokes his head into her home, she pushes her powerful bottom at him. She wedges his head and body between the warren walls and her rump. **OOMPH!** The fox quickly wriggles away and runs off into the forest.

Over the next few weeks, the wombat continues her nightly routine. She digs and digs, building tunnels to connect the new chamber with her original warren. Sometimes she lies on her side and scratches at the roof and walls of the warren to make it bigger. If any roots are in her way, it's not a problem! **SNAP** – she bites them off with her sharp teeth. She also gathers twigs and leaves to line her sleeping chamber.

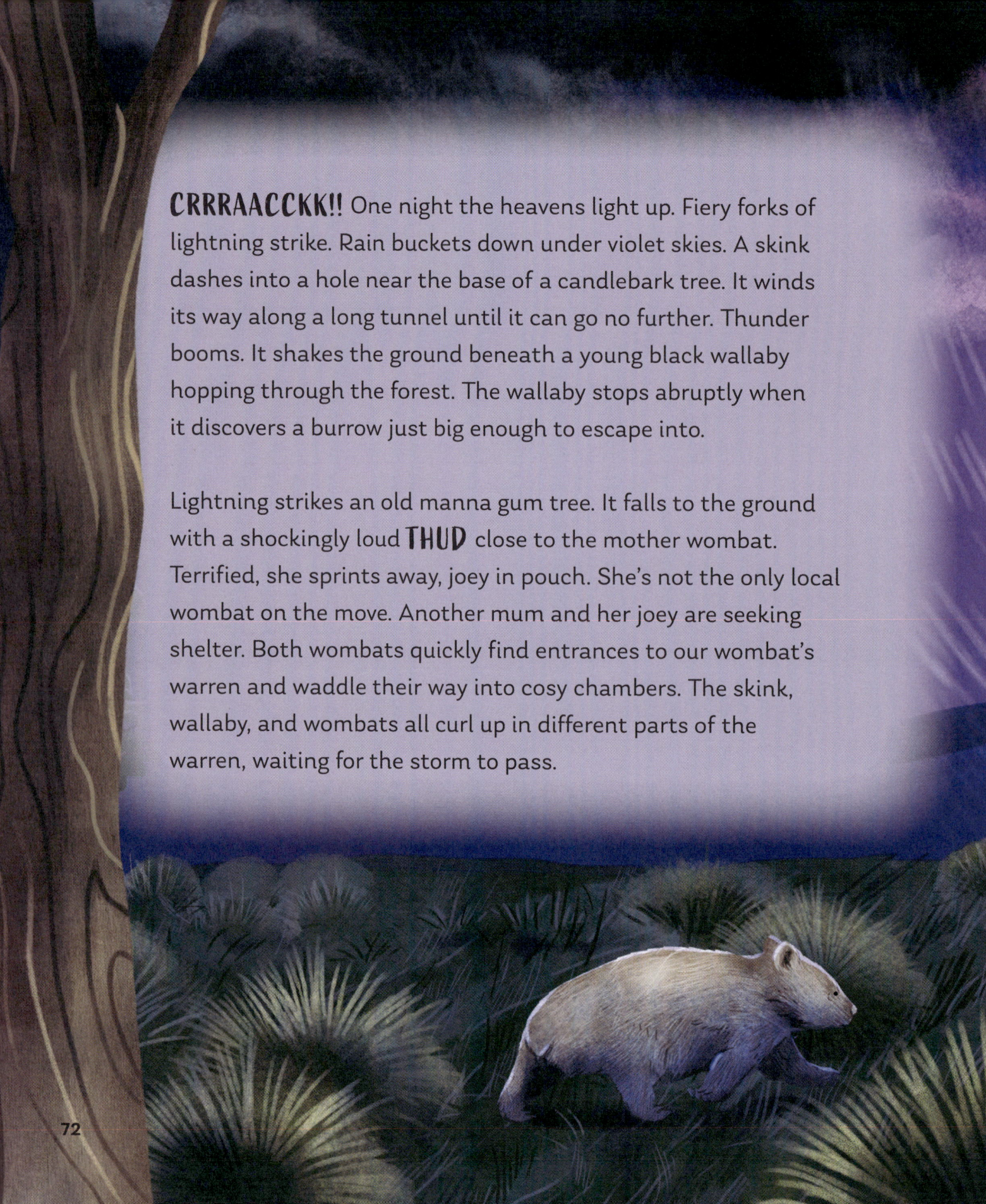

CRRRAACCKK!! One night the heavens light up. Fiery forks of lightning strike. Rain buckets down under violet skies. A skink dashes into a hole near the base of a candlebark tree. It winds its way along a long tunnel until it can go no further. Thunder booms. It shakes the ground beneath a young black wallaby hopping through the forest. The wallaby stops abruptly when it discovers a burrow just big enough to escape into.

Lightning strikes an old manna gum tree. It falls to the ground with a shockingly loud **THUD** close to the mother wombat. Terrified, she sprints away, joey in pouch. She's not the only local wombat on the move. Another mum and her joey are seeking shelter. Both wombats quickly find entrances to our wombat's warren and waddle their way into cosy chambers. The skink, wallaby, and wombats all curl up in different parts of the warren, waiting for the storm to pass.

THE SCIENCE BEHIND THE STORY

A Friendly Burrower

Bare-nosed wombats, sometimes known as common wombats, are native to Australia. They are one of the world's largest burrowing animals. Adults are the size of a medium-sized dog. The ones in this story live in Wombat State Forest in the Australian state of Victoria.

Marvellous marsupials

The wombat, koala, and black wallaby in this story are all marsupials, a type of mammal. So are kangaroos. Marsupials have pouches where their babies, called joeys, develop and grow. Unlike other marsupials, wombats have rear-facing pouches. This prevents joeys from being covered in dirt when their mums dig – lucky wombats!

Wombats sometimes sleep on their backs with all four feet in the air!

Tremendous teeth

The teeth of bare-nosed wombats grow throughout their lives. Gnawing on bark helps wombats wear down their teeth. Their vegetarian diet includes grasses, sedges, mosses, plant roots, and tubers.

Poo cubes

A wombat's cube-shaped poo looks different from almost any other animal poo you will ever see. The shape is created by the wombats' digestive system. They have an extra-long colon and their digestion process is quite slow. Wombats leave about 80–100 droppings per day. That's a lot of poo!

Sharing is caring

Wombats pay visits to one another's burrows from time to time. When hiding from predators or escaping fires or bad weather, a variety of animals also share wombat warrens. These include wallabies, skinks, rabbits, bettongs, and even little penguins.

A Wild Winter Chase

The Kola Peninsula in Russia is a winter wonderland in December. Snow blankets the Arctic tundra in a seemingly endless sea of white. The sun never rises during this period of polar night. At first glance, one might think that nothing much happens here. Yet surprises abound in this magical landscape…

A small shock of red appears from a patch of crowberry bushes. It's the dramatic eyebrows of a rock ptarmigan! He walks slowly over the snow without sinking in, thanks to his feathered feet. Another ptarmigan soon emerges from the same bushes. One eats some twigs. The other finds some purple saxifrage. **PECK!** That hits the spot.

Unbeknownst to the ptarmigans, another tundra bird is thinking about food. A snowy owl is perched on a dwarf birch tree. The owl slowly turns his head. He looks to his right, to the back, and finally to his left. His piercing yellow eyes hone in on a possible meal – one of the rock ptarmigans!

In a flash, the snowy owl silently swoops down. He grabs one of the ptarmigans with his talons and takes flight. Oh, no! Both ptarmigans make a series of anxious clucking sounds.

The bird caught in the owl's talons flaps his wings wildly. After a terrifying couple of moments, the victim manages to escape the owl's clenches! He zooms towards a mountain pass with the owl in hot pursuit. That is until the predator spots an easier target. Peeping out of a hole in the snow is a Norwegian lemming. Flapping fast through the bracing air, the owl changes his flight path. The lemming is much more likely to be an easy meal… or so he thinks.

Just as the owl dives down to snatch the lemming, a white streak blazes across the tundra. It's nearly impossible to see, but an Arctic fox is running after the lemming! Our owl has competition. The fox closely follows the rodent's every twist and turn. Meanwhile, the owl keeps pace with the lemming. He hovers right above it, ready to strike.

At that exact moment, the fox pounces, catches the lemming, and runs off with his prize. Better luck next time! Hunger drives the snowy owl on. He flies low over the tundra, scanning for signs of life. The winds **WHIP** across the open landscape. They scatter the glittering snow in the dim light. Without warning, an ermine pops out from a hidden den.

Sensing the owl above, the ermine bolts, **SCREECHING** around frosted rocks and low shrubs. In a wild twist, a wolverine appears on the scene and joins the chase. The owl is just ahead, and swoops low to grab the ermine. But the wolverine is fast. It quickly catches up to the owl. Frantic, the owl just manages to take off before the wolverine pounces. The wolverine steals the ermine. How rude!

A snowstorm has begun. After three unsuccessful hunts, our owl heads back towards his perch at the base of the Khibiny Mountains. His luck finally changes when another Norwegian lemming appears. The owl quickly snatches this one. He **GULPS** it down, headfirst, in one go. Then he settles down for a rest. Though a thick layer of snowflakes soon coats his feathers, he isn't cold. Light, steady flurries continue to fall, glowing in the twilight. After the thrill of the chase, the snowy owl can barely keep his eyes open. He drifts into a deep sleep...

THE SCIENCE BEHIND THE STORY

What a Hoot!

Snowy owls are often found on the Arctic tundra, though some migrate in winter to areas further south. They are one of the heaviest owls because of their many feathers, which keep them warm. These birds weigh roughly the same as three basketballs!

Male or female?

In the Harry Potter books, the snowy owl Hedwig is female. However, in the movies, male snowy owls were used to play her part. This is because males are whiter than females. Females have a salt-and-pepper appearance, due to the black and brown markings on their feathers.

Female

Spit it out

Owls swallow small prey whole and larger prey in big pieces. However, owls can't digest bones, teeth, fur, or feathers. These leftover parts of prey are compressed into a pellet that the owl then spits out. Owls usually cast out one pellet each day.

Polar night

While most owls are active at night, snowy owls are usually active during the day. But this story is set in the dark because each winter the Kola Peninsula has a period known as polar night. For most of December and part of January, the sun never rises. So it's dark all of the time.

Lively lemmings

Many animals in the Arctic tundra have colouring that helps them blend in with their environment. The snowy owl, rock ptarmigans, Arctic fox, and ermine in this story all do. But Norwegian lemmings are different – they have bold colours that stand out against the snow.

Male

Snowy owls can turn their heads almost the whole way around!

Learning from the Expert

In the cool hours before dawn, a mother honey badger and her cub move through the miombo forests of Mozambique. Red oat grass **CRUNCHES** beneath their feet. The honey badgers hope to find a bee's nest. The mum stops and turns her head upwind. Not a hint of honey in the air...

Continuing on, the honey badgers pass an aardvark. It's ambling towards a huge termite mound, ready to gorge itself on the insects inside. The mother has more important things on her mind, like the bird's nest she has spied up ahead. It's the nest of a bird called an Angola pitta. Inside are eggs that must have broken when the nest fell to the ground. The mother and her cub hungrily tuck in to the tasty yolk.

The honey badgers are crossing a dried-out stream bed when the ground beneath them starts to shake. **BOOM! BOOM! BOOM!** A herd of elephants is trampling along in search of water. The elephants aren't interested in the honey badgers. However, they could easily be crushed underfoot. The mother climbs a nearby julbernardia tree. Her cub, a quick learner, follows suit.

When the heavy footsteps of the elephants cease, the mum teaches her cub how to find food in the forest. She digs along their path and shows the youngster a variety of roots and bulbs. Things are going smoothly until a small pack of African wild dogs approaches. Normally, the dogs would be snoozing at this hour, but the bright moon has them on the prowl. The dogs creep closer. The pack is only feet away from the honey badgers now. Will they escape these fearsome hunters? It's two versus five.

The mother honey badger makes a **RATTLING** noise. Her cub **SQUEAKS** faintly. Then the mum takes action. She drops a stink bomb right under the noses of the dogs. *PEE-YUW!* What a stench! The pack turns tail, rushing away from the stink.

The early morning sunlight bathes the trees in a golden glow. Daybreak brings new sounds to the miombo forest. A pale-billed hornbill greets the day with repeated piping whistles. **PI-PI-PI-PI-PI-PIEU-PIEU!** Impalas weave between the trees, chewing grass and crushing dry leaves with their hooves. Meanwhile, the honey badgers are still on their quest for honey.

The mother stops suddenly. She sniffs and catches the faintest whiff of her favourite food. She and her cub follow the sweet scent – past sable antelopes, past a Hildegard's buff butterfly, and below a brown-hooded kingfisher on the wing. Suddenly, the smell of honey is strong. The honey badgers arrive at a giant baobab tree. And wedged into the tree's trunk is a huge bee's nest!

The mother quickly scales the tree and **RIPS** into the nest with her sharp front claws. As she breaks the nest open, bees swarm out. They attack the mum, but she doesn't give up. Her thick skin provides some protection from the painful stings. Her cub joins her to eat the chewy, sweet waxcomb and the larvae inside. However, it isn't long before the stinging bees become too much of a distraction for the cub. It runs off not too far away until the bees are no longer chasing it.

A few minutes later, a greater honeyguide discovers the leftovers from the honey badgers' breakfast. The brown-and-gold bird pecks at the wax, then carries off a chunk to enjoy later.

The intense morning sun heats up the miombo forest. Mum and baby honey badger are ready to head to bed. With full bellies, they return to their hidden home in a hole beneath a horn-pod tree. There they both curl into balls, ready for the sweetest of dreams.

THE SCIENCE BEHIND THE STORY

Smelly, Strong, and Savage

Honey badgers are native to parts of Africa, from southern Morocco to the continent's southern tip. They are also found in some areas in Asia. The ones in this story live in the miombo woodlands of northern Mozambique.

Stink bomb

Honey badgers store a smelly liquid at the base of their tails. They use this to mark their territory or to drop "stink bombs" when they're afraid or threatened. Even though the smell doesn't last very long (unlike a skunk's spray), it sends a message: *leave me be!*

A special woodland

Miombo woodlands spread across much of southern and central Africa. This habitat includes open woodlands, as well as savannahs, tropical grasslands, and shrubland. Miombo woodlands are home to a huge variety of wildlife, including rhinos, giraffes, lions, and some of the biggest elephant populations in Africa.

Sweet deal

Honeyguides lead people to bees' nests and both species benefit from this cooperation. The humans can harvest the honey and the birds eat the honeycomb that's left over.

Venomous snakes can make up to 25% of a honey badger's diet.

Make yourself at home

Honey badgers use their long, sharp claws to dig their burrow homes. These burrows are made up of one tunnel leading to a sleeping chamber. Honey badgers will also sometimes take over the burrows of other animals.

Afraid of nothing

Honey badgers are famed for their bravery. They will even take on leopards and lions. They eat venomous snakes, including cobras and puff adders. Luckily, they have a strong resistance to snake venom.

Who Glows There?

A red-tailed tropicbird glides over coral islands in the Indian Ocean. It gradually dips down,
                down,
                      down,
                            until its feathers skim the water's surface. There, it will bob and rest during the night.

In the distance, the sun is on the horizon. Although the evening sky is full of colour, so too is the reef below. A school of purple queens swims above staghorn coral. Some bicolour parrotfish graze on algae. While a crown-of-thorns starfish is crunching on hard coral, a large humphead wrasse creeps closer and closer. Then… **SNAP!** The starfish becomes a snack.

As darkness falls, nocturnal marine creatures start to appear. Manta rays sweep over the reef. Their fins smoothly undulate. Up and down. Up and down.

Something else appears on the scene. It looks like a piece of fruit. It seems to be a... pineapple! Has this delicious yellow treat been dropped by tourists exploring the reef? It would be highly unlikely, given how few people come here each year. But wait a second! This pineapple seems to have fins. That's not a fruit at all – it's a young Australian pineapplefish!

The pineapplefish is not a strong swimmer. She slowly makes her way towards the seafloor. **POP! POP! POP!** Three little garden eels poke their heads out from the sandy sea bottom. They sway like grass in the breeze, watching the young pineapplefish as it tootles along.

A bright green light illuminates the seafloor. No divers are around this remote reef tonight, so where could the light possibly be coming from? The pineapplefish's lower jaw is glowing like a torch! Thanks to this built-in light, she quickly finds some shrimp. She **CHOMPS** down and continues to explore.

Meanwhile, above the waves a meteor shower is putting on quite the show. One meteor after another streaks across the sky. Back on the reef, something else is streaking along. It's a tiger shark. *Uh-oh*. It looks like the shark has set its gaze on our pineapplefish. It gains on her. Fearing for her safety, the pineapplefish closes her mouth. Quick! Turn off the light! Her green glow disappears instantly. *Phew* – that was close! The puzzled shark heads off in pursuit of other prey instead.

Once the coast is clear – **PING** – the pineapplefish lights up again. During her nighttime ramblings, she passes a shipwreck among the shoals. She also spies a sea turtle and giant clams. All the while, the pineapplefish's light helps her find food. Sometimes she uses her light to communicate with other pineapplefish, but the messages they exchange remain a mystery.

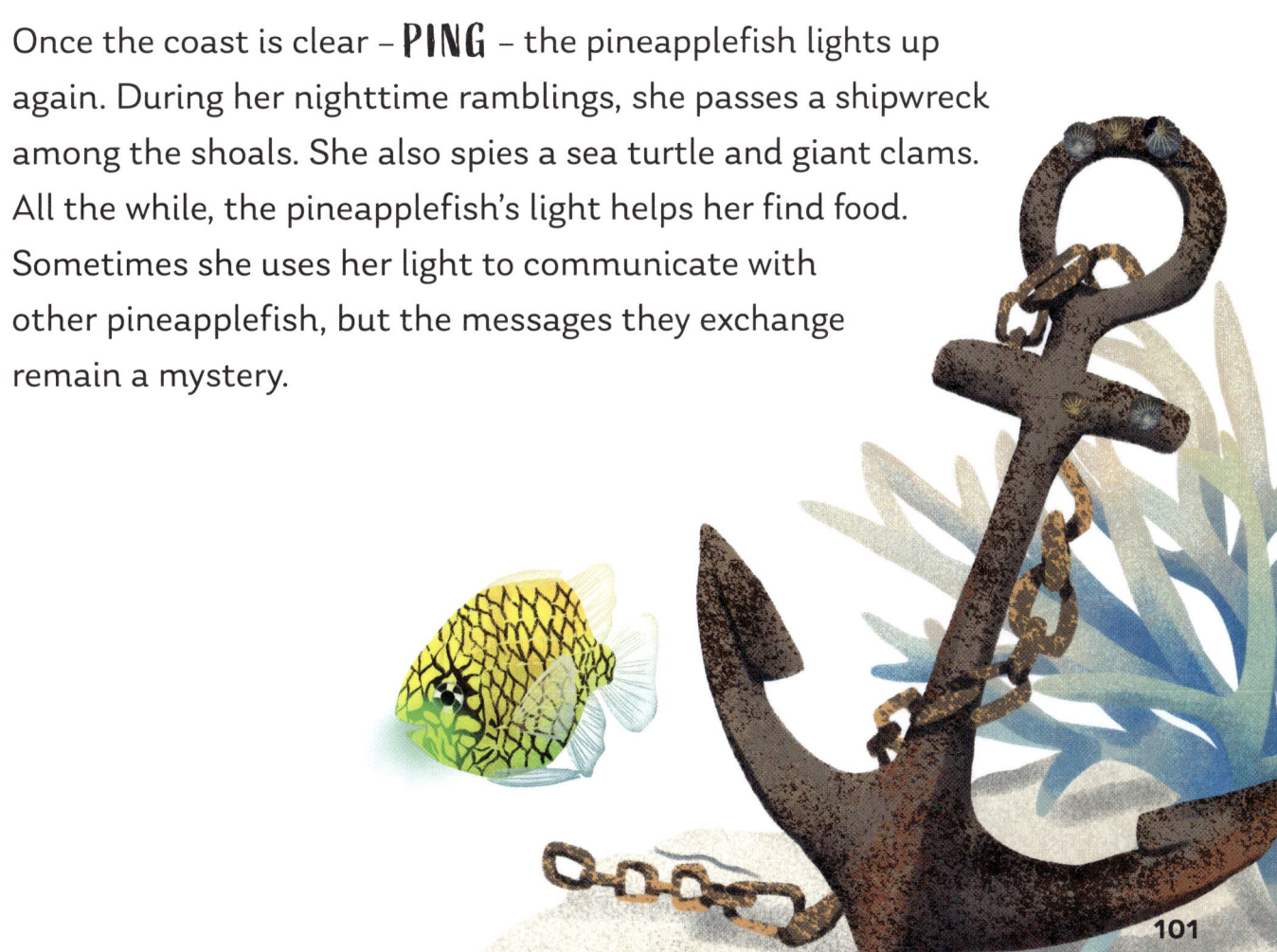

Just before dawn, a huge potato grouper swims past. Colourful cleaner wrasses pop in and out of its wide-open mouth, giving its teeth a good brush! When a dogtooth tuna approaches, the grouper snaps his jaws. This tells the tuna: BACK OFF! Meanwhile, the pineapplefish makes its way home.

The pineapplefish is nestling back in the reef when an octopus's arm pokes into the nooks and crannies around it. Startled, she pushes herself deep into the coral reef. Luckily, the octopus doesn't find our little friend and moves on in search of dinner. The pineapplefish decides to call it a night. She drifts off to sleep inside the cavernous coral she calls home.

What's in a name?

Pineapplefish are named for their prickly skin and bright yellow scales that give them a similar appearance to pineapples. Some people call them knightfish because their rough scales resemble chain-mail armour that medieval knights wore in battle.

Life on the Reef

Australian pineapplefish are found along the east and west coasts of Australia. Rowley Shoals Marine Park is home to the pineapplefish in this story. The park is located in the Indian Ocean off Australia's northwest coast.

Hide-and-seek

Pineapplefish use their light to attract prey. Scientists think they might also use the light to communicate with other pineapplefish, but they haven't deciphered these cryptic messages yet. If a pineapplefish's light catches the attention of a predator by mistake, they can shut it off by closing their mouth.

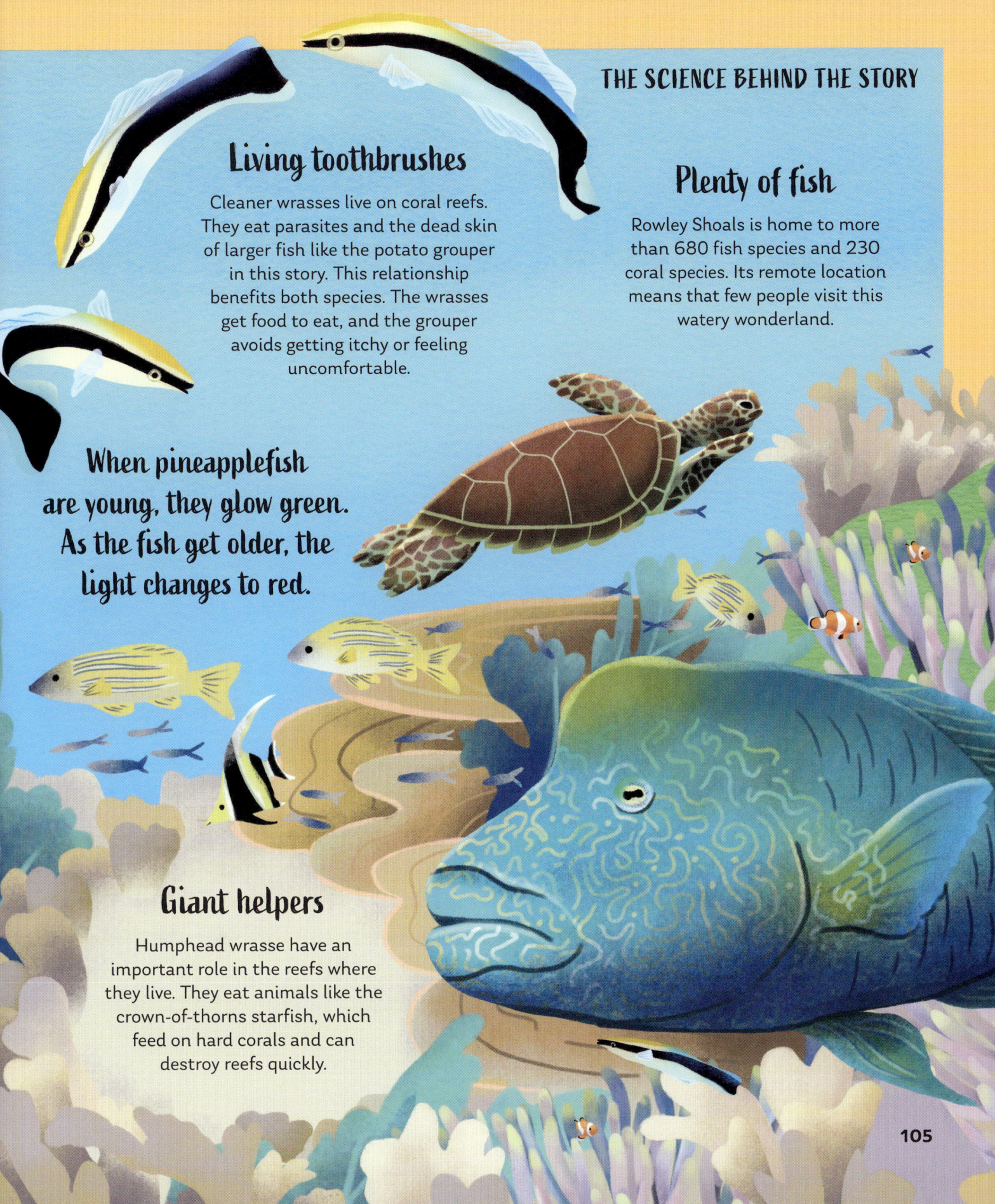

THE SCIENCE BEHIND THE STORY

Living toothbrushes

Cleaner wrasses live on coral reefs. They eat parasites and the dead skin of larger fish like the potato grouper in this story. This relationship benefits both species. The wrasses get food to eat, and the grouper avoids getting itchy or feeling uncomfortable.

Plenty of fish

Rowley Shoals is home to more than 680 fish species and 230 coral species. Its remote location means that few people visit this watery wonderland.

When pineapplefish are young, they glow green. As the fish get older, the light changes to red.

Giant helpers

Humphead wrasse have an important role in the reefs where they live. They eat animals like the crown-of-thorns starfish, which feed on hard corals and can destroy reefs quickly.

Blooms at Bedtime

High above the Sonoran Desert in North America, the night sky is awash with shades of blue. Bright stars and the glowing Milky Way make the heavens look even more magical. Down below, the silhouettes of giants loom over the rocky soil below. Despite their tall bodies and long arms, these giants are not scary. They are huge saguaro cacti!

Peeking out from a hole within a cactus is a tiny elf owl. It scans the landscape for predators like ringtails and bobcats. Not seeing any threats, it swoops down to ground level. It grabs a beetle first, then nabs a spider. **CRUNCH**. On the way back to its hidden home, the owl passes bulbous green buds on top of many of the saguaro cacti.

It's nearly midnight when one of the saguaro buds starts to bloom. As the bud bursts open, a large white flower unfurls. Inside its waxy petals is a bright yellow centre. Another blossom on the same cactus opens up just moments later. They fill the air with the most incredible scent. It smells like ripe melons.

The delicious smells travel on the wind, attracting creatures of the night. A lesser long-nosed bat soon arrives. Its muzzle reaches deep inside the saguaro blossom. Before long, the bat's hairy little head is covered with pollen.

A second bat appears on the scene. This one is a Mexican long-nosed bat. The bat heads to the top of a saguaro arm where another flower has just opened. **SLURP!** Like a hummingbird, the bat hovers in flight to feed on the nectar. What a sweet feast!

Before long, the first rays of sunlight shine over the desert. A herd of javelinas starts their day in the cool early morning. They **SNORT** as they forage for agave hearts, roots, and cholla flowers. They are delighted to discover a patch of prickly pear cactus. It's one of their favourite foods. But before they dig in, **STOMP! STOMP! STOMP!** They flatten the spines on the cactus pads to make them easier to swallow.

More daytime creatures rise and shine. Some head to the saguaro blossoms. A white-winged dove flies swiftly towards the melon-scented blooms. Its wings **WHIR** and **WHISTLE** in flight. The dove moves from one flower to the next, reveling in their nectar and pollen.

Higher up on the same saguaro, a gila woodpecker is drumming against the cactus's thick, pleated flesh. Carving out a hole in the saguaro is hard work, but it will pay off when the woodpecker's future chicks have a safe place to grow. Far below, a rarely seen gila monster dashes across the desert floor.

Even though they only just bloomed, time is ticking for the saguaro flowers. They only have a few hours left before they close forever. Honey bees waste no time. They **BUZZ** amid the blooms, pollinating the blossoms in the flowers' final hours. Next year, more saguaro flowers will enchant the desert with their scent and beauty all over again.

THE SCIENCE BEHIND THE STORY

Desert Giants

Long lives

Saguaros live for about 150 to 175 years. Biologists think some may even reach more than 200 years old. These cacti grow slowly. They produce their first flowers at around 35 years old. One saguaro cactus can have as many as 100 flowers on it in a season.

Saguaro cacti are the tallest cacti in North America. They can grow to be 15 m (50 ft) tall – that's the same height as a five-storey building! The cacti in this story are growing in Arizona's Saguaro National Park, which is located within the Sonoran Desert.

From flowers to fruit

In June and July, the pollinated saguaro flowers change and grow into juicy red fruits. Animals spread the seeds of these fruits through their poo. From some of the seeds, new saguaro cacti will grow. Decades later, new saguaro flowers will bloom and the cycle will continue.

Save it for a dry day

It's not easy to find water in the desert. The roots of a saguaro cactus allow it to soak up as much moisture as possible after a rare heavy rain. When this happens, the pleats in the cactus's body expand like an accordian. A woody skeleton inside the cactus supports its heavy weight.

Fleeting flowers

Each beautiful, highly scented bloom of a saguaro cactus opens up at night and is gone by the next afternoon, less than 24 hours later. Nighttime pollinators of these flowers include bats and moths. Birds and bees pollinate them in the morning.

The Pizza Heist

A taxi beeps its horn. A busker toots a tune on her saxophone. A fire engine blares its siren. **NEE-NAW, NEE-NAW**. All these sounds make for a loud late-night atmosphere. That's no bother for a certain city dweller. Despite the ruckus, a Norway rat climbs out from beneath a dumpster.

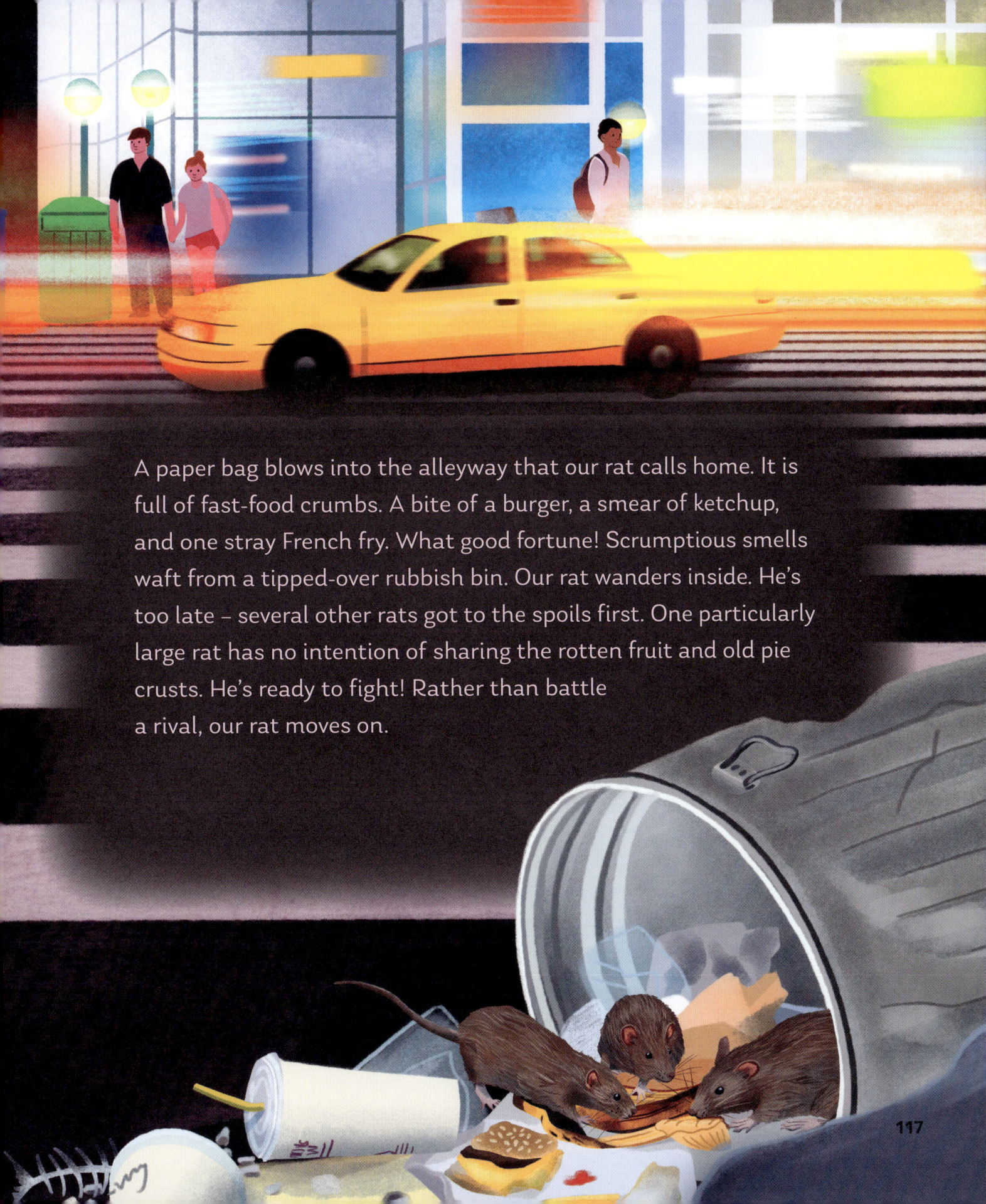

A paper bag blows into the alleyway that our rat calls home. It is full of fast-food crumbs. A bite of a burger, a smear of ketchup, and one stray French fry. What good fortune! Scrumptious smells waft from a tipped-over rubbish bin. Our rat wanders inside. He's too late – several other rats got to the spoils first. One particularly large rat has no intention of sharing the rotten fruit and old pie crusts. He's ready to fight! Rather than battle a rival, our rat moves on.

The rat gnaws and nibbles his way along the dark passage. He clambers over enormous piles of rubbish. Finally, he arrives at the end of the alleyway. He briefly looks up at his surroundings. Though he cannot see all the amazing colours that humans can, he can tell that it's dizzyingly bright. Giant neon signs light up the night. Our Norway rat is standing in the middle of New York City's Times Square!

The rat doesn't have long to take in the scene. Shoes of every style **WHIZZ** past him. All pose a threat to the small night-time wanderer. After more than a year living here, the rat knows people don't want him around. He's been chased with a broom and nearly flattened by a skateboarder. His tail has been stepped on numerous times. And once, a pizza delivery person sped after him on their bike for several blocks.

Speaking of pizza, the rat's keen sense of smell tells him some is near. He stands on his hind legs and sniffs deeply. He scurries over to where half a slice of a delicious pepperoni pizza has been dropped. His long, sharp front teeth sink into it. Before anyone can steal his loot, he runs off, carrying it down the stairs of a subway station. The slice hits each step on its way down.

Suddenly, a shoe sends him – and his pizza – flying. The rat lands very close to the train tracks. **TOOOOOT! TOOOOOT!** A train is speeding into the station! The rat hurriedly pulls his prize off to the side. After his close call, he savours the cheesy slice in his trackside hideaway.

As the night goes on, it gets quieter as the trains run less often. The rat finds a coin-sized hole in the wall, where interesting smells lure him from inside. He puts his head through then pulls it back. His body is much wider than the tiny hole. There's no way he can get through. Unless… He pops his whiskers through the hole again. This time, he shimmies and squeezes his whole body through. He's in!

Inside the wall, our rat climbs along heating ducts and old pipes. **TIP, TAP, TIP, TAP**. Occasionally he lucks out and discovers various crumbs: a chocolate-covered coffee bean, a few sunflower seeds. They might have come from a café in the station or an apartment high above. The rat is not a picky eater so almost anything is fair game. He makes a mental map of this location so he can return to enjoy its food again in the future.

After hours of exploring the inside of the walls in the train station, the rat is ready to go home. **SNIFF, SNIFF**. When he gets a whiff of fresh air from a hole, he wiggles his way through. He's not far from his nest. He runs along the edge of the pavement. *Eeeek!* An early morning street cleaner catches sight of him. She pushes the rat with her broom… right into a drain! The rat drops deeper and deeper below the city. **SPLASH!** He finally plops down in the sewer system.

After navigating his way through a maze of pipes, our rat looks out at New York Harbor. He swims through the dark water. Eventually, he reaches a marina. It's nearly dawn. He scrambles up a buoy, speeds along a gangway, and races across a rope leading to a large ship.

The rat explores the ship, seeking out a place to rest. He settles in a storage room beneath a mishmash of boxes. Not bad for a hiding spot! The ship will soon sail away. Will our rat end up in London or Singapore? Only time will tell.

THE SCIENCE BEHIND THE STORY

A tight squeeze

Rats are famous for being able to fit through small spaces like pipes or holes in walls. They can do this because of the way their bodies are built. Their ribs are hinged at the spine and can collapse to make the rat's body smaller. So when they push through a tiny space, it's no trouble at all.

A Creature of Many Talents

Norway rats are also known as brown rats, common rats, sewer rats, and wharf rats. Despite their name, they are native to northern China. Today they are found on every continent except Antarctica.

Super swimmers

Even though rats are land animals, they do well in water too. They can tread water for three days straight! They can also hold their breath underwater for a whopping three minutes. Talk about super stamina!

Where's the cheese?

Rats have an excellent memory. Once they discover a place with a regular food supply, they will remember it and make a mental map of how to get there.

Norway rats are colour-blind.

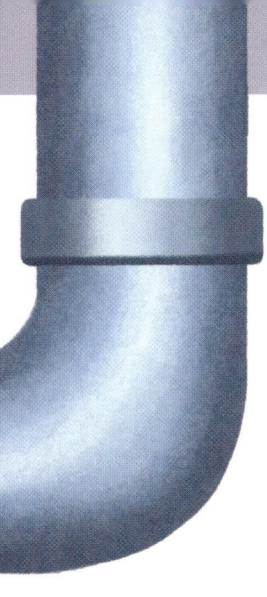

Eating local

Rats typically don't travel far from home in search of food. In fact, they rarely travel more than 100 m (330 ft) from their nest in a single night.

I'll eat anything!

Norway rats are not picky eaters. They eat anything that people eat, as well as many things we don't (such as animal poo). Scientists once looked inside a rat's stomach and found more than 4,000 different items!

The Night Flight

The afternoon sun lights up the canopy of a paper birch tree. It's early June in Saskatchewan, Canada. Way down on the forest floor, red squirrels chatter as they search for seeds. A Canada jay spies an old mushroom, swoops down, then takes off with its tasty treasure between its feet.

In the leaf litter, a precious little bundle is wrapped up in some of last autumn's leaves. **SHHHH...** do you hear a rasping sound? It's coming from inside the cocoon. The very soft saw-like noises continue. Then, with an almighty **CRACK**, the cocoon splits open. A luna moth pops out to greet the world for the very first time!

When the moth emerges from the cocoon, her wings are small, crumpled, and wet. She is not ready to fly yet. Her fragile new body needs to adjust to life outside the cocoon. Gingerly, she scales a nearby tree. It's time for nature to take its course.

The luna moth is a shape shifter in the hours to come. Her wings unfold and lengthen. Her swollen abdomen shrinks. The new moth also needs time to dry out since she can't fly with wet wings. She must wait while, all around her, life in the forest continues as normal. A group of cedar waxwings pass by, diving after dragonflies mid-air.

As night falls, the moth takes to the sky. The moon is almost full. The insect's seafoam green wings are hard and dry now. She flies through the forest with grace and beauty. She is lucky when a hungry barred owl finds a mouse to eat, instead of her. **SNAP!** The owl grabs its dinner then returns to its perch. A grass spider catches an insect in its web among the grass. Although many nocturnal animals are hunting and eating, the luna moth is not. She just flits to and fro in the night.

The following day, the luna moth hides among the bright birch leaves. A yellow-bellied sapsucker lands right next to her. The moth's camouflage is a great shield against predators. The bird **PECKS** at the tree trunk. The sapsucker may have missed a moth meal, but it slurps up sap and trapped bugs.

After twilight, the luna moth releases a chemical into the air. The scent travels on the wind, attracting males from miles around. The males' wide, feathery antennae detect the smell. Several suitors zigzag though the air, flying as fast as they can. They can't wait to find the source of the scent.

The first male arrives. The full moon illuminates the courting couple. The very next night, the female starts to lay eggs. She lays a few under the leaf of a birch tree. Then she glides to an aspen tree and lays another small cluster of eggs. With hundreds of eggs to lay, it will take more than one night to finish the job.

A few nights later, after her final delivery, the luna moth is heading back to the tree where she was born. All of a sudden – **SWOOSH** – a bat appears and dives towards her. She spins her long twisting tails as she flies, confusing the bat. The moth escapes, just in the nick of time. Settling on her tree, she knows that in a few days her eggs will begin to hatch.

THE SCIENCE BEHIND THE STORY

Life cycle

An adult luna moth is only alive for one week. However, a lot happens before they even hatch. Let's find out how they transform from tiny eggs to beautiful insects.

Stage 1 – Adult luna moths lay hundreds of eggs on leaves.

The Circle of Life

Luna moths are native to North America. They are one of the biggest moth species on the continent. Their wingspan is typically bigger than a baseball!

Stage 2 – Tiny caterpillars, or larvae, hatch from the eggs 7–13 days later.

Stage 3 – The young caterpillars spend 3–4 weeks eating and growing. As they get bigger, they shed their skin. This is called moulting.

Master of disguise

Luna moths can hide in plain sight thanks to how they look. Their green wings provide camouflage in clusters of leaves. Some edges of their front wings are reddish-brown, making them look like twigs. As if that wasn't enough, eyespots on all four wings often confuse predators.

Stage 5 – The adult moth emerges from its cocoon and the cycle starts again.

Stage 4 – Inside its cocoon, the caterpillar turns into a moth in a process called metamorphosis.

Nothing on the menu

Because the luna moth has a very short life, it can survive without food. It doesn't even have a mouth! It lives on fat that it stored when it was a caterpillar.

Hide-and-Seek

A blue-headed pitta calls out **PPOR-WI-IIL**. It digs up a few ants from the rainforest floor just before twilight. It is about to nab a last bug before bedtime when it nearly steps on a pile of poo. *Eew*! The bird hops around the disgusting mess, eats a beetle, and flies off to roost for the night.

With no moon in the sky, it's soon pitch black. For a moment, the forest is almost quiet. The only sounds are red leaf monkeys chomping on leaves above, while giant centipedes and a Malayan tarantula are zigzagging around the foliage below. Suddenly, the speckled poo begins to move! How is that even possible? What the blue-headed pitta thought was a pile of poo is actually a young Wallace's flying frog!

The frog has been lying still all evening, waiting for his chance to move without being noticed. Now that the coast is clear, he hops off to catch insects with his sticky tongue. A Bornean angle-headed lizard spies the frog, but our young friend has nothing to worry about – the lizard is waiting for its own bug feast.

A kukri snake senses the frog nearby. In a flash, it **SLITHERS** down the trunk of a kamala tree. No time for foraging now! The frog leaps between the thick roots of a binuang tree. Though the young frog is not old enough to glide away from the snake, his quick footwork helps him escape.

For more than a year, the young frog disguises himself as poo. By day he rests on giant leaves as orangutans feed on fruits and chestnuts nearby. By night he catches mosquitoes while bats ambush moths overhead. Sometimes his hopping gives his true identity away, but the frog's creative camouflage turns away many predators. He won't have this superpower for very long. Soon he starts to change dramatically. Black webbing develops between his toes. Skin flaps appear on his arms and legs. His skin becomes much smoother. His spots disappear. The adult frog is now a brilliant emerald green.

The adult frog moves to a new habitat. He now lives high up in the rainforest canopy. Here barringtonia blooms open at night, releasing their sweet scent. The frog looks on as small bats and moths stop by the flowers. Raindrops bounce off leaves during the many afternoon showers.

RROH-RROH! RROH-RROH! A rhinoceros hornbill takes off from a fig tree. It is en route to its roost for the night. But when it glimpses the frog, its plan changes. The bird's wide ebony wings flap as it races in the frog's direction. Our amphibian athlete heads to the end of a branch before – *wheeee!* – the frog takes a bold leap. His four legs stretch out as if he were a flying superhero. The loose skin flaps on his arms and legs catch air as he flies through the forest until he lands on the trunk of a fig tree with a thump. His large toe pads stick to the bark. The frog scrambles to find a hiding spot among the leaves where he can be safe.

There's a pattern to the Wallace's flying frog's life in the canopy. He rests during the day and goes on foraging adventures at night. The frog glides between trees regularly. One time, a red giant flying squirrel soars past as the frog is pursuing a spider.

The frog also leaps for love. One day, after torrential rain, the frog glides down to the forest floor. He adds his call to the cacophany of sounds from other frogs that fill the air. A female is on a low branch near a pool close by. She seems to be sitting among a pile of foam. Our frog heads in her direction. They mate, then go their separate ways.

In the weeks that follow, their eggs grow and change. Tadpoles develop inside until one day... **PLOP! PLOP! PLOP!** The next generation of Wallace's flying frogs splash down into the pool below. What adventures does the forest hold in store for them?

THE SCIENCE BEHIND THE STORY

Beware: Flying Frogs

Wallace's flying frogs are native to Southeast Asia. They are typically found in tropical forests. These amazing amphibians can glide as far as 16 m (52 ft) when leaping between trees. The ones in this story live in the Danum Valley on the island of Borneo.

Juvenile

Moving home

When a Wallace's flying frog is young and looks like poo, it dwells in the lowest layer of the rainforest. That's where the poo of birds and bats (which can be red with white speckles) ends up. As an adult, the frog lives in the treetops where its bright green colour blends in with the leaves.

Hose pygmy flying squirrel

Tadpoles

Gliding buddies

The Danum Valley is home to other animals that soar through the air. Hose's pygmy flying squirrels, red giant flying squirrels, and colugos all glide from tree to tree here.

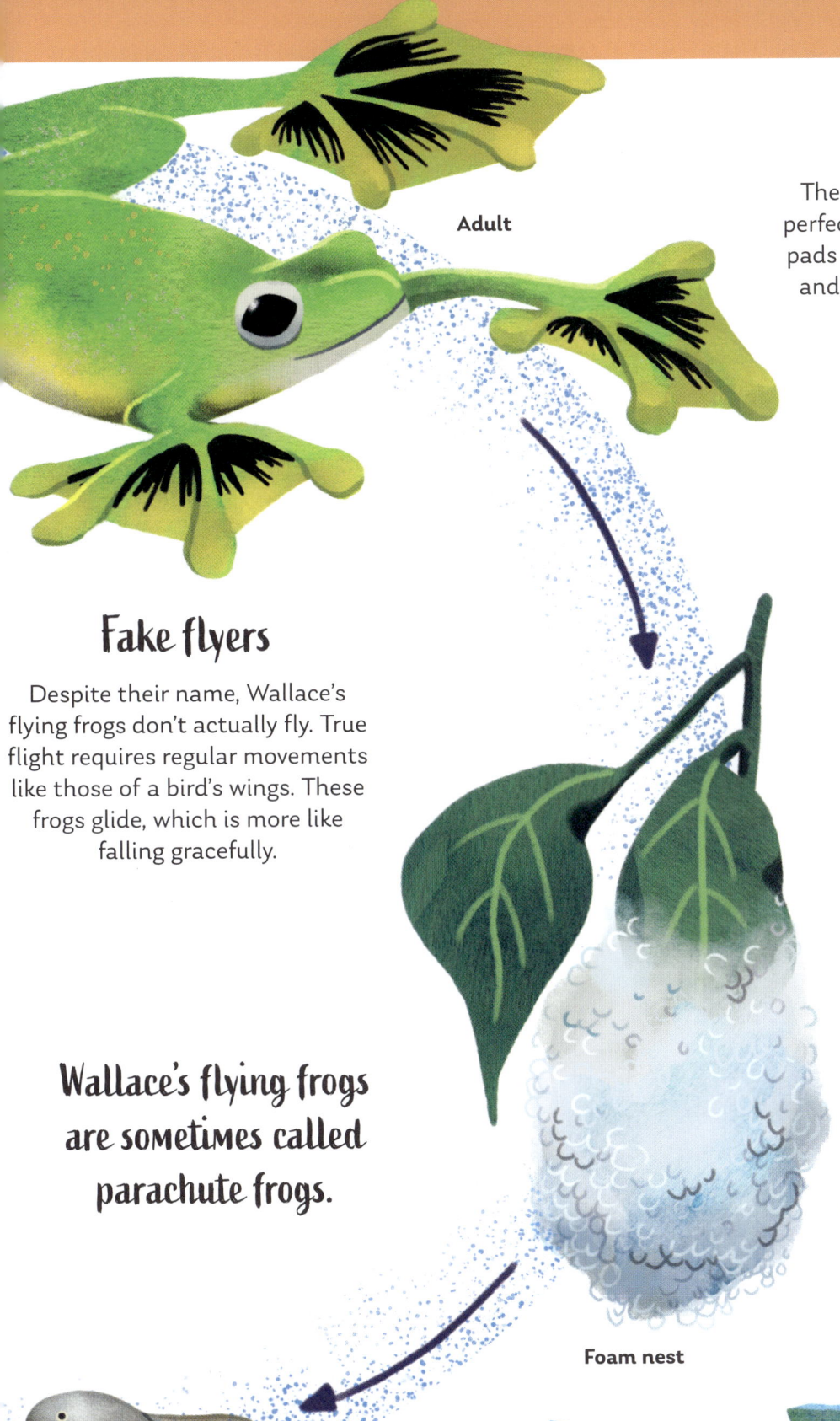

Adult

Terrific toes

The toes of Wallace's flying frogs are perfect for acing a landing. Their big toe pads allow them to land softly on trees and help the frogs stick to the trunk. Toe-tally awesome!

Fake flyers

Despite their name, Wallace's flying frogs don't actually fly. True flight requires regular movements like those of a bird's wings. These frogs glide, which is more like falling gracefully.

Wallace's flying frogs are sometimes called parachute frogs.

A foamy beginning

Female Wallace's flying frogs create foam nests where they lay their eggs. Unlike most frogs that lay their eggs *in* water, Wallace's flying frogs lay them *over* water. When the tadpoles hatch, they fall into the water where they can continue to grow and have the moisture they need to survive.

Foam nest

The Bushbaby Babies

A bushbaby family wakes up as the sun is setting. The mum pokes her head out from the hollow of a mopane tree. She rotates her ears, listening for danger. Deciding all is well, she emerges from her home. Her daughter comes out of the nest. A furry set of twins follows. And then another set of twins! All these bushbabies fit in the tree hollow because they're tiny!

Just like people, they take a little time to get going. They yawn and stretch. Each of the fuzzy family members grooms themselves. One youngster paws his head. Another cleans her ears. **SLURP, SLIP**. A third sibling spruces up the fur on his neck.

All of a sudden, the mum **WHISTLES** loudly. She's warning her family that an eagle is flying through the surrounding woodlands. The youngsters must stay put until the danger passes.

When the coast is finally clear, the mother bushbaby and her children all head out in different directions. Given how far every leap takes them, they are soon scattered throughout their woodland home. What adventures does each bushbaby have? Let's find out!

The oldest sister is a pro at whizzing through the woods. As she leaps from one mopane tree to the next, she passes over an elephant family resting. She grabs a moth mid-air then alights on a leafy branch. **CRUNCH!** She munches the moth before moving on quickly in search of her next bite to eat.

One of the older twins arrives at an acacia tree. A wad of sweet, juicy gum is oozing from the bark. The bushbaby laps it up in a flash. Then she hops from branch to branch, hoping to discover more sugary sap on this tree. Her keen sense of smell leads her to a deep crack in an upper limb. She sticks her narrow, rough tongue inside and is rewarded with a delicious treat.
SLUUURRPPP!

Later that night, another loud whistle grabs the attention of the bushbaby family. One of the younger twins is sounding the alarm this time. She'd just gripped a mopane trunk when a terrifying sight loomed overhead. A predator called a genet saw her and was coming her way! Time for a split-second departure. The teeny bushbaby pulls back her ears to pass between some thorny acacia trees. Luckily the gap is too small for the genet to fit through. Relieved, the bushbaby stops to rest in the crook of a leadwood tree.

The young bushbaby's alarm call puts her siblings on high alert. They hear a Pel's fishing owl making a deep, horn-like **OOOM** sound. A porcupine gnaws on some bones during his nightly roam. Neither of these animals causes much concern. However, small creatures can never be too careful in the forest at night.

A few minutes later, one of the younger twins sniffs, detecting a familiar smell similar to his own. It's his older brother! They chirp and click at each other, before taking a break from finding food to play a game of tag. Launch. Land. Launch. Land. What fun! Thanks to their sticky feet, they grip the trees easily.

SQUEAK! SQUEAK! After spying a rock python nearby, the mother bushbaby sounds another distress call. Her five babies race back to the tree where their evening began.

After all the excitement and drama, it's time for some relaxation. The bushbabies groom each other as the sun starts to peek over the horizon. Then they climb into the tree hollow nest for a good day's rest.

THE SCIENCE BEHIND THE STORY

Petite Primates

There are at least 20 species of bushbabies, also known as galagos. The ones in this story are southern lesser galagos. They are about the size of squirrels and are native to several countries in southern Africa. The bushbaby family in this story lives in the Okavango Delta of Botswana.

Big families

The first time a female bushbaby gives birth, she usually only has one baby. But after that first time, she is more likely to have twins. She can give birth twice a year.

Eye see you

A bushbaby has very large eyes that help it see in low light, which is important since they are active at night. A bushbaby's eyes are so large that they fill up their entire eye sockets. Bushbabies cannot move their eyes like we can. Instead, to look around, they turn their whole head. Luckily, they can rotate their heads 180 degrees.

Bushbabies can visit as many as 500 trees in a single night!

Useful wee

Both female and male bushbabies wee on their hands in a behaviour known as "urine washing". They wipe their wee-covered hands on other members of their family. This helps to strengthen their bonds. When the bushbabies move from tree to tree, the wee on their hands also helps to mark their territory. And it may give them a better grip on the trees. Who knew wee could be so useful!

Leggy leapers

Bushbabies have powerful hind legs, with very large muscles and stretchy tendons. These allow them to catapult themselves between trees super quickly!

Glossary

Algae
A group of underwater organisms, which vary in size and colour. They are neither plants nor animals. But like plants, they get their energy from the Sun. Seaweed is one type of algae.

Amphibian
A cold-blooded animal that lives in the water when it is young, but can live on land as an adult. Toads, frogs, salamanders, and newts are amphibians. Unlike birds and reptiles, amphibian eggs are usually laid in water.

Biologist
A scientist who studies living organisms, such as plants and animals.

Cactus
A type of plant with spines or scales instead of leaves.

Camouflage
The natural form or colouring of an animal that allows it to blend in with its surroundings.

Cocoon
A silky case that is spun by many young insects to protect themselves before they become an adult.

Den
A wild animal's resting or living place.

Hatchling
A young animal, which has recently come out of its egg.

Joey
The name given to young kangaroos, koalas, and other marsupials. Joeys are often carried in a pouch on their mother's tummy.

Juvenile
A young animal that looks like an adult but is smaller and can't yet have babies.

Marsupial
A type of mammal that includes kangaroos, wombats, opossums, and koalas. Marsupials are different from other mammals because their babies mostly develop in a pouch outside of their mother's tummy.

Metamorphosis
A series of big changes that some animals undergo as they change from an immature form to an adult form, for example a tadpole changing into a frog.

Migration
The seasonal process where some animals move from one region to another to have babies or in search

Moult
To shed old feathers, hair, skin, or even a shell to make way for new growth.

Nest
A structure a bird makes (or sometimes a place it chooses) to lay its eggs in and raise its young.

Nocturnal
A word that describes animals that are active at night.

Parasite
An animal or plant that lives on or inside another animal or plant. Parasites gain benefits from this relationship, but their hosts do not!

Pellet
A wad of undigested material (such as fur and bones) regurgitated by a bird.

Polar night
A period of time in the polar regions when the Sun does not rise above the horizon for over 24 hours.

Pollination
The act of transferring pollen from the male parts of a plant to the female parts of a plant, which creates seeds.

Predator
An animal that catches, kills, and eats other animals.

Prey
An animal that is caught, killed, and eaten by another animal.

Reptile
A cold-blooded animal with scales that reproduces by laying eggs. Crocodiles and lizards are examples of reptiles.

Rodent
The family of animals that includes mice, squirrels, and beavers. Rodents have constantly growing incisor teeth!

Tundra
A vast, treeless region found in the Arctic and subarctic regions of North America, Europe, and Asia. It has permanently frozen subsoil and vegetation consisting of lichens, mosses, herbs, and dwarf shrubs.

Warren
A network of interconnecting burrows, such as those made by wombats or rabbits.

Index

A
aardvarks 86
acacia trees 150
African dung beetles 26–35
alligators 21–25
amphibians 136–145
anoles 19
antelopes 91
Arctic tundra 84
astronomy 34, 45
Australia 74, 104
Australian pineapplefish 98–105

B
badgers 86–95
banyan trees 6, 9, 11, 13
baobab trees 91
barringtonia 140
bats 6–14, 19, 108–109, 133, 144
bees 91–92, 95, 113
beetles 25, 26–35
birch trees 78, 126, 132
birds 36–45, 78–85
Borneo 144
Botswana 154
buntings 36–45
bushbabies 146–155
butterflies 91

C
cacti 106–115
Canada 57, 64, 126
caterpillars 134–135
centipedes 136
clams 101

claws 95
click beetles 25
cocoons 135
Colombia 39, 40, 44
coral reefs 96–97, 103, 105

D
dances 35
dens 46, 55
doves 111
dragonflies 127
dung beetles 26–35

E
eagles 148
ears 55
eels 99
eggs 42, 132, 134, 145
egrets 17
elephants 88–89, 148
ermines 61, 81–82, 85
Everglades National Park 16, 24
eyes 24, 154

F
feathers 44, 84
feet 54, 95, 145
fennec foxes 46–55
fish 96–105
flying foxes 6–15
flying frogs 136–145
foxes 15, 46–55, 70, 80–81
frogs 17, 18, 68, 136–145
fur 54

G
galagos 154
genets 150
gila monsters 111
grey wolves 56–65
groupers 102, 105

H
herons 22
honey badgers 86–95
honeyguides 93, 95
hornbills 90, 141
howls 64
hyenas 31

I
impalas 90
India 6, 14
Indian flying foxes 6–15
Indian Ocean 96, 104
indigo buntings 36–45
insects 26–35

J
javelinas 110
jays 126
jerboas 52
joeys 66–69, 72, 74

K
kangaroos 74
kingfishers 91
knightfish 104
koalas 68, 74
Kola Peninsula 76, 85

L

lemmings 62, 79–81, 83, 85
Libya 54
life cycles 134–135, 144–145
lizards 19, 55, 137
luna moths 126–135

M

maps 4–5
marsupials 74
megabats 14
Mexico 39, 44
microbats 14
migration 36–45, 84
miombo woodlands 86, 90, 94
monkeys 136
mosquitoes 19, 139
moths 126–135, 139
Mozambique 86, 94

N

New York City 118, 122
nocturnal animals 4–5
Norway rats 116–125

O

octopuses 103
Okavango Delta 154
owls 51, 78–85, 107, 128, 152

P

parachute frogs 145
parrotfish 97
pellets 84
pig frogs 17
pineapplefish 98–105
pittas 86, 136
polar nights 85
pollination 14, 108, 113, 115
poo 26–35, 75, 115, 139
porcupines 152
primates 154
ptarmigans 57, 77–78, 85

R

rats 116–125
rays 97
reptiles 22–25
Rowley Shoals Marine Park 104–105
Russia 76, 85

S

saguaro cacti 106–115
Sahara Desert 46, 54
sapsuckers 130
scorpions 49–50
sharks 101
skinks 72, 75
smells 94
snakes 52, 95, 139, 152
snowy owls 78–85
songs 45
Sonoran Desert 106, 114
South Africa 26, 35
squirrels 126, 142, 144
starfish 97, 105
stars 45

T

tadpoles 142, 144
teeth 24, 25, 75
termites 86
tropicbirds 96
tuna 102
turtles 101

U

United States of America (USA) 24, 39, 44, 114
urban habitats 116–125

V

Vancouver Island 38
venom 135

W

wallabies 72, 74, 75
Wallace's flying frogs 136–145
warrens 70–72, 75
waxwings 127
wee 155
wild dogs 89
wings 15, 135
wolverines 82
wolves 56–65
wombats 66–75
woodpeckers 111
wrasses 97, 102, 105

Y

Yukon 57, 64, 65

Z

zebras 26–27, 34
zilla 48

This has been a
NEON SQUID
production

To Pete, Lily, Cadi, and Simon, my favourite stargazing companions. Whether spying satellites from our deck or watching shooting stars on our rural road in upstate New York, I love exploring the night skies with all of you. Hope you all get to see many more celestial wonders in the years to come!

Author: Alicia Klepeis
Illustrator: Jennifer Falkner
Consultant: Dr Brittney G. Borowiec

Editor: Malu Rocha
US Editor: Allison Singer
Proofreader: Joseph Barnes
Indexer: Elizabeth Wise

The author would like to thank the following experts for their help:

Dr Baheerathan Murugavel
Dr Eric Warrant
Dr Jessica van der Wal
Dr Marie Dacke
Dr Stephen T. Emlen
Dr Susi Stückler
Dr Ulmar Grafe
Mark McGrouther
Ranger Trent Seale

Copyright © 2025 St. Martin's Press
120 Broadway, New York, NY 10271

Created for St. Martin's Press
by Neon Squid
The Smithson, 6 Briset Street,
London, EC1M 5NR

EU representative: Macmillan Publishers Ireland Ltd,
1st Floor, The Liffey Trust Centre,
117–126 Sheriff Street Upper,
Dublin 1, D01 YC43

10 9 8 7 6 5 4 3 2 1

The right of Alicia Klepeis to be identified as the author of this work has been asserted in accordance with the Copyright, Designs and Patents Act 1988.

All rights reserved. No part of this publication may be reproduced, stored in a retrieval system, or transmitted, in any form or by any means (electronic, mechanical, photocopying, recording or otherwise), without the prior written permission of the publisher.

A CIP catalogue record for this book is available from the British Library.

Printed and bound in Guangdong, China by Leo Paper Products Ltd.

ISBN: 978-1-91674-505-6

www.neonsquidbooks.com